ELLIOTT CARTER

HBHH

for Solo Oboe

T0079358

HENDON MUSIC

First performed on May 27, 2007
in Ittingen, Switzerland by Heinz Holliger

NOTE FROM THE COMPOSER

HBHH was composed for the 68th birthday of the great oboist, composer and dear friend.

In German scores our B-natural is H and our B-flat is B.

— Elliott Carter

HAPPY BIRTHDAY HEINZ HOLLIGER
(B)   (B♭)   (B)   (B)

HINWEIS DES KOMPONISTEN

HBHH wurde anläßlich des 68. Geburtstages des großartigen Oboisten, Komponisten und sehr geschätzter Freund komponiert.

In deutscher Musikschreibweise wird das internationale B als H und das B-flat als B geschrieben.

— Elliott Carter

HAPPY BIRTHDAY HEINZ HOLLIGER
(B)   (H)   (B)   (B)

NOTE DU COMPOSITEUR

HBHH fut composé à l'occasion du 68ème anniversaire de l'éminent hautboïste et compositeur, mon cher ami Heinz Holliger.

Selon la notation musicale germanique *si* naturel est noté H et *si* bémol est noté B.

— Elliott Carter

HAPPY BIRTHDAY HEINZ HOLLIGER (HBHH = si-si♭-si-si)
(JOYEUX ANNIVERSAIRE HEINZ HOLLIGER)

Duration: ca. 3 minutes

for *Heinz Holliger*

HBHH

Elliott Carter
(2007)

979-0-051-09843-9

Printed in USA
First Printed 2021

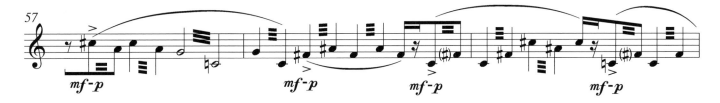